This Book is Presented to:

_____

By:

_____

Date:

_____

The ABC Bible Storybook

Karen Ann Moore

Illustrated by Beeky Farley

A Faith Parenting Guide can be found on page 94.

Dedicated to:

The wonderful woman
who gave me my first Bible when I was five,
my great-grandmother — Jenny Crance.
K.A.M.

Faith Kids™ is an imprint of
Cook Communications Ministries, Colorado Springs, CO 80918
Cook Communications, Paris, Ontario
Kingsway Communications, Eastbourne, England

THE ABC BIBLE STORYBOOK
©2000 by Karen Ann Moore for text and Becky Farley for illustrations.

Faith Kids™ is a registered trademark of Cook Communications Ministries.

All Scripture is taken from the *Holy Bible, New International Version*. Copyright © 1973,1978, 1984 International Bible Society. Used by permission of Zondervan Bible Publishers.

Edited by Jeannie Harmon
Designed by iDesignEtc.

First printing, 2000
Printed in China
04   5 4 3 2

Library of Congress Cataloging-in-Publication Data

Moore, Karen Ann, 1050-
   The ABC Bible storybook/Karen Ann Moore; illustrated by Becky Farley.
   p. cm.
   Includes bibliographical references.
   ISBN 0-7814-3390-8
   1. Bible stories, English. 2. English language--Alphabet--Juvenile literature. [1. Bible stories. 2 Alphabet.] I. Farley, Becky, ill. II. Title.

BS551.2.M66 2000
220.9'505--dc21

                                    00-039363

Table of Contents

Table of Contents (cont)

Let's read stories
from A to Z
To share God's love
for you and me.

A is for Adam

Adam was first
    with his wife, Eve,
Who taught us
    to listen to God
    and believe.

He showed us what happens
    when we go astray
And try to live life
    our very own way.

For when Eve met the serpent
    in the garden of glory,
Things quickly changed
    in the human life story.

Eve ate the fruit,
    for she was deceived
And forgot in a moment
    all she believed.

And once she had eaten,
    Eve knew good and bad
And the very big difference
    between happy and sad.

When Adam ate too,
    they lost all their joy
And things that they never
    knew they could destroy.

They left the sweet garden
  to work in the land,
Missing out on the life
  God so dearly had planned.

Poor Adam and Eve
  were totally blind
To all of the love
  God meant them to find.

Let's learn from the story
  of Adam and Eve,
And be faithful to God
  and all we believe.

You can read the real Bible story in Genesis 2 and 3.

B is for Brothers

B is for brothers
born moments apart,
Who struggled to win
their father's heart.

One son was Esau,
covered with hair
The other was Jacob,
somewhat more fair.

Jacob, the younger,
was loved by his mother,
While Isaac favored
the hunter, his brother.

Cooking a stew
one fateful night
Helped Jacob to win
his brother's birthright.

For Esau was hungry
and in just the right mood
To give all that he had
for some good, hearty food.

In one foolish moment,
he swore that he'd give
His brother his birthright
for as long as he'd live.

Some years later
> when their father had aged

Another deceit
> was cleverly staged.

Isaac was ready
> to bless his son's name

Once he prepared
> some savory game.

But Rebekah heard
> old Isaac's request

And hoped that Jacob
> would be the one blessed.

So Jacob pretended
> that he was his brother

To deceive his father
> and please his mother.

Adding some fur
> to his own smooth hand

He created the meal
> he so cleverly planned.

Since Isaac was blind
> he fell for the plot

And blessed Jacob's life
> right there on the spot.

Then when Esau returned
    with meat and some dressing,
He went to his father
    to ask for his blessing.

Poor Isaac was troubled;
    he trembled severely;
He had nothing left
    for the son he loved dearly.

"I've given the blessing
    to Jacob," he said,
"And it will forever
    remain on his head."

Esau was angry;
    his brother had lied,
And feeling the sadness,
    he broke down and cried.

Then Esau went one way
    and Jacob the other
Until time would heal them
    as brother to brother.

If you have a brother
    or sister or two,
Remember to share
    all that God's given you.

Read the real Bible story in Genesis 25—27.

C is for Commandments

When the children of Israel
    left Egypt behind,
They traveled the desert
    a little bit blind.

They didn't quite know
    the way to God's land,
But they knew that He led them
    by His gracious hand.

God gave them manna
    and He gave them quail,
And watched over them all
    so His plan would not fail.

They often complained;
    they just didn't see
That a little more trust
    would set them all free.

Moses, their leader,
    taught them to pray
And watch for God's hand
    leading their way.

Approaching Mt. Sinai,
    the children were still
While Moses met God
    on top of the hill.

At first they were patient,
     but soon were in fear
And forgot what they knew,
     without Moses near.

They took all their gold
     and melted it slowly
And made a great calf
     that they thought was holy.

When Moses returned
     from the mountain top,
He was angry and caused
     all the dancing to stop.

He broke the stone tablets
     he meant to deliver —
The special commands
     of God, the Law-giver.

But finally, each rule
     was delivered and heard
And the Ten Commandments
     became God's precious word.

And still to this day
     we all do our best
To keep the commandments
     that make our lives blessed.

Read the real Bible story in Exodus 19—20

D is for Disciples

Disciples are people
    who follow the lead
Of someone who teaches
    them things that they need.

Now Jesus had followers,
    twelve in all,
Who traveled with Him
    and answered His call.

First, there was Simon,
    called Peter, the brother
Of Andrew, who answered,
    becoming another.

The third and fourth
    were Zebedee's sons,
Named James and John,
    both special ones.

Then there was Philip,
    Bartholomew, too,
Who followed Jesus
    as the number grew.

Thomas, the doubter,
    yet strong in his way,
And Matthew the tax man,
    not liked in his day.

James, son of Alphaeus,
and Thaddaeus, too,
Were chosen by Jesus
to be part of the crew.

Then, finally, came Simon
from Galilee's coast,
And Judas Iscariot,
who betrayed Him the most.

And with these twelve men,
Jesus started to teach
All who would listen
and all He could reach.

He taught them of God
and showed them the way
That they could be saved
and be His every day.

And we are disciples
of this Jesus too
When we follow Him
in the things that we do.

For He's chosen us
just like He did then
To go and tell others
He's always our friend.

Read the Bible story in Matthew 10.

E is for Earth

God formed the earth
    with nothing in sight.
He said to Himself,
    "Let there be light!"
He created this planet
    and gave it birth,
And filled it with treasures
    of unbelievable worth.

He created the heavens,
    the stars shining bright,
Created the daytime,
    and moon for the night.
He created the flowers, the plants,
    and the trees,
And all of the fish
    that inhabit the seas.

He created more things
    than we've ever seen.
He made the skies blue
    and the tall grasses green,
And then He created
    a gardener or two;
He created dear ones
    like me and like you.

He told us back then,
    and He tells us today,
Take care of the earth
    in your work and your play.
Make it a place
    where my flowers can grow,
And make it a place
    to reap what you sow.

For as children of God,
     we all play a part
In making the earth
     His true work of art.
We need to remember
     that we have a hand
In keeping the earth
     the way that God planned.

Read the creation story in Genesis 1.

F is for Faith

Hebrews eleven
    gives us a view
Of all that faith
    is meant to do.
It is faith that helps us
    really receive
God's own truths
    in which we believe . . .

By faith
    we believe in all God created,
By faith
    we see Cain and the brother he hated.
By faith
    we know Enoch was not made to die,
By faith
    Noah answered without asking why.
By faith
    Abraham talked to God face to face,
By faith
    Sarah had a son by His grace.

By faith
  baby Moses was saved by the king's
  daughter.
By faith
  Pharaoh's army all died in the water.
By faith
  all the walls of Jericho fell,
And by faith
  God chose Rahab and saved her as well.

So all these examples
  are good to recall
Because it's by faith
  that God saves us all.

Read the faith chapter in Hebrews 11.

G is for Grace

Saint Paul, in his letters
    often sent grace
To the people of God
    in some distant place.

He offered them peace
    and offered them hope,
For he wanted to give them
    a new way to cope.

The new way was grace,
    God's gift through His Son,
That promised new life
    and new strength to each one.

We hear the word grace
    in a good Sunday sermon,
But getting its meaning
    may be hard to determine.

Grace means that God
    forgives all our sin
And helps us to grow
    and begin again.

The Bible reminds us
    that we all receive it
The moment we hear
    God's truth and believe it.

We stay strong in the grace
     of Jesus, our Lord,
And through God's mercy
     we are always adored.

When you hear about grace
     from a teacher or friend,
Then give God the praise
     and the thanks there and then.

For we live every day
     in great joy and peace,
In God's constant love
     and His grace that won't cease.

*Read more about grace in
Romans 1, 3, 6, and 11.*

H is for Hope

Now hope is an interesting word,
    yes, indeed,
And it's one that we use
    when we each have a need.

We hope for good things
    day in and day out;
We ask and we pray
    and we try not to doubt.

When the Bible shares hope,
    it defines it this way:
That our hope is in Jesus,
    day after day.

Our Living Hope,
    the Son, most High,
Brings us hope
    to live and try.

We might hope for a swing,
    a new doll, or a toy,
Because hope gives us reason
    to find all of life's joy.

So whatever you wish for,
    or hope for, or pray,
Remember that Jesus
    brings hope for each day.

Read about hope in Romans 5 and 8.

I is for Idol

God's people were told
    to stay away
From idols worshiped
    in their day.

But Shadrach, Meshach,
    and Abednego,
Were told by the king
    that they must bow low.

But they said, "No!"
    They would not be told
To worship an idol
    made of gold.

So the king sent the three
    to the fiery flame
Where they all continued
    to worship God's name.

And God saved the men
    with His angel of light,
And the king knew his idols
    had no power or might.

Little children,
    the Bible goes on to say,
Keep yourselves from idols
    all through the day.

Read Daniel 3 for a better understanding of idols.

J is for Joseph

The sons of Jacob
      thought him wise
      and loved him like no other,
But they were jealous
      of the way
      Jacob loved their brother.

Joseph was the eleventh son
      and favored by his dad,
But when he got a brand-new coat,
      his brothers all got mad.

They didn't think it funny,
  and they didn't think it nice,
That Joseph always got new things,
  but they just got advice.

Joseph told them of his dreams,
  of seeing shafts of wheat
That seemed to all bow down to him
  and lay right at his feet.

This made his brothers angry,
  so they decided then and there,
To send poor Joseph far away,
  even though it wasn't fair.

At first they put him in a pit
  where they thought he would die,
But then they sold him as a slave
  when a caravan drove by.

The brothers thought that now they'd
  have their father's love and joy,
But they didn't know how much he'd
  grieve at losing his dear boy.

So years went by and Joseph lived
  in Pharaoh's mighty court,
And he controlled the grains that fed
  the people from each port.

Famine hit the desert land,
    and people from the plain
Went to Joseph and the King
    to try to buy some grain.

The brothers went to Egypt too,
    to get grain and supplies,
And Joseph recognized them
    but he kept it a surprise.

He gave them what they needed,
    then said, "Go your way.
Bring me your youngest brother
    and let this other brother stay."

The brothers were alarmed at this
    but honored his command
And left to find young Benjamin
    back in their father's land.

At last, when they returned again
    With Benjamin at their side,
Joseph couldn't hide the love
    he'd always kept inside.

"I'm your brother Joseph,
    blessed by God's own hand
To care for all His people
    when the famine hit the land.

God worked everything for good,
    and we are surely blessed.
So I forgive you, Brothers,
    and give you Egypt's best."

They all rejoiced to once again
    be family and friends,
And so you see how happily
    this special story ends.

Remember God has good in mind
    in everything you do,
For He wants you to be someone
    who blesses others too.

Read more about Joseph in Genesis 37, 39—47.

K is for Kings

The Bible speaks of many kings,
　　and lists them all by name.
Let's look at just a few of them
　　for they weren't all the same.

Some of them were very good
　　and followed God each day,
But some of them were very bad
　　and just went their own way.

One great king was David
　　who really became known
For killing old Goliath
　　with a slingshot and a stone.

David tried to follow God,
　　and that's what made him strong,
And when he slipped along the way,
　　God forgave all he did wrong.

Solomon was David's son;
　　Bathsheba was his mother,
And Solomon ruled Israel
　　with wisdom like no other.

He settled everyone's disputes;
    he gave each one advice,
And even the Queen of Sheba
    thought he was pretty nice.

He built a brand-new temple
    to worship the true Lord,
And God blessed him with riches
    as an honor and reward.

The kings of Israel were great;
    some had lasting fame,
But none can match the King of Kings —
    and Jesus is His name!

*Read about David in 2 Samuel and Solomon
in 1 Kings.*

L is for Light

"Let there be light."
    God spoke the words
    to bring the light of day
And in that one bright moment
    chased the darkness all away.

God spoke of light
    and placed the sun
    near the earth's own sphere,
And then He made the moonlight, too
    and made the stars appear.

God made the light
    to shine for us
    and help us understand
That everything on earth responds
    to His great command.

Then, when Jesus
    walked on earth,
    He shared another view,
For Jesus said the brightest light
    comes from me and you.

"You are the light,"
    Jesus said
    to those he came to know,
"And you must live in a way
    that lets your own light show."

So when you see
    the stars above
    or look out at the sun,
Give God thanks and praise and love
    for all that He has done.

Then think of all
    the special things
    that you alone can do
And know how much it pleases God
    when your own light
    shines through.

*Read Matthew 5:14-16 to see Jesus' words
about light.*

M is for Mary

A young and faithful woman
        was God's own chosen one
To be the loving mother
        of His only precious Son.

An angel came to visit her
        and told her heaven's story:
That she would be the one to bear
        the King of Kings and glory.

She thought about the things
        she heard and kept them in her heart,
And prayed to understand it all
        and humbly do her part.

She thought about dear Joseph,
        whom she was pledged to marry,
And wondered how to tell him
        about the baby she would carry.

But God took care of everything
        and told Joseph His plan too,
For He knew Mary needed him
        to carry this plan through.

And from here you know the story
of the stable and the manger
Where the precious Son of God was born,
protected from all danger.

And Jesus honored Mary,
and blessed His mother too,
And this is an example
of what He wants you to do.

Read about Mary in Luke 2.

N is for Noah

Noah was a righteous man
    who walked with God each day.
He raised his family in God's sight
    and taught his sons to pray.

Now you may think
    that everyone should worship
    and obey,
But sadly, that was not the truth
    in old Noah's day.

For no one seemed to follow God
    or try to seek Him out,
So God took matters in His hands,
    and here's what came about.

He talked with His friend, Noah,
    and told him of a plan
To flood the earth and wash it clean
    of all the sins of man.

God said, "I'll save you, Noah,
    and your sons and their wives, too,
And this is what I have in mind
    that I want you to do.

Build an ark, a place to stay,
    and I will be your Guide.
I'll help you build it safe and warm
    and put animals inside.

Take every kind that you can find,
    male and female of each breed,
And take some food and some supplies
    for every special need.

And I'll be with you day and night.
    You'll be safely in My hand,
And then I'll lead you once again
    to a promised land."

So Noah did all the things
    God wanted him to do.
He built the ark and filled it up
    with animals, two by two.

And after forty days of rain
    and many days afloat,
God helped them find a brand new land
    where Noah docked his boat.

What can we learn from Noah
    that still is true today?
That when God calls, answer Him,
    "I hear, Lord, and obey."

Read the story of Noah, beginning in Genesis 6.

O is for Oil

Jesus told a story
    about five women who were wise,
Who filled their lamps with oil
    and kept more in their supplies.

And then He also mentioned
    five women who were scared,
Because all their oil had run out
    and they were not prepared.

These maidens waited day and night
    for the bridegroom to appear,
And though they waited patiently,
    he never came quite near.

The maidens all grew weary,
    and soon they fell asleep,
And when the bridegroom finally came
    the maids began to weep.

For their oil was all gone,
    and the way was dark and dreary.
They couldn't find the bridegroom,
    for they all were pretty weary.

So the five without the oil
    begged the five who had it all,
But the maidens soon discovered
    no one there to heed their call.

The bridegroom took the ready maids
and then he shut the door,
And the maids who'd lost their oil
all went out to buy some more.

When they returned to join him
they asked to come inside,
But he answered "I'm so sorry,
I've already got my bride."

So the maids without the oil
were sad as sad could be,
And this is where the story starts
to talk to you and me.

For it says that we all need to be
prepared and very steady,
For when our Lord returns to earth
we all need to be ready.

For we are like the maidens
storing oil every day,
Getting ready for our bridegroom,
Jesus Christ, to come our way.

Read the story Jesus told in Matthew 25:1-13.

P is for Paul

The story of Paul
    helps us to see
How God always knows
    what we can be.
For God took Paul
    and made him blind
Until he changed
    his heart and mind.

For Paul was known
    for bringing blame
To those who loved
    Jesus' name.
Until the day
    God set him right
And helped him see
    the blessed light.

Once Paul changed,
    he changed for good
And preached of all
    that he understood
Of Jesus' grace
    and Jesus' glory—
Telling others
    God's great story.

Paul wrote letters
    to his friends
Of the grace
    God always sends,
And he traveled
    far and wide
All around
    the countryside.

Once he took
>a dangerous trip
In a storm
>that wrecked his ship,
And though
>it caused quite a scare,
It gave Paul
>even more to share.

Paul wrote to churches
>of his day
And tried to help them
>on their way.
He sent his love
>and Jesus' grace
To everyone
>from place to place.

Paul even spent
>some time in jail,
But still his mission
>didn't fail
For he was always
>strong and ready
To show God's love
>is true and steady.

So we, like Paul,
>can try each day
To share God's grace
>in some kind way
And show the world
>that we know too,
That Jesus' love
>is always true.

Read more about Paul, starting with Acts 9.

Q is for the Queen of Sheba

There were some
     in ancient days
Who lived in all
     the grandest ways.
Their palaces
     were fit for kings,
And so they treasured
     many things.

Now Solomon,
     who was so wise,
Had a palace
     of great size.
He had vast fortunes,
     and his gold
Was almost more
     than could be told.

Stories of his wealth
     and blessing
And riddles
     he was always guessing
Made a Queen
     long to see
If what she heard
     could really be.

So the Queen of Sheba
        made a plan
To visit
        with a caravan.
Of gold and treasures
        from her store,
To see which one
        of them had more.

You can be sure
        she was impressed.
The king had more
        than she had guessed,
And when she left,
        she gave him praise
For his wisdom
        and godly ways.

And still today,
        if we are wise
We'll see the good things
        God supplies
As His way
        of bringing treasure
Beyond anything
        that we can measure.

*Read about Solomon and
The Queen Sheba in 1 Kings 10.*

R is for Ruth

61

When we need an example
of goodness and truth,
It serves us all well
to think of Ruth.
For Ruth was a woman
so humble and fair
That her story is something
quite special to share.

When Ruth and Naomi
each lost their spouse,
They decided to move
to a new land and house.
Naomi chose
to go back to the place
To see her own family again—
face to face.

Because she loved Ruth,
just like her own,
She offered to go to her people
alone.
For Naomi knew
Ruth was not of her race
And might stay a widow
and live in disgrace.

But Ruth would not hear it;
she simply said, "No,"
And, "Wither thou goest,
there, too, shall I go."
So Ruth was determined,
and Naomi was blessed,
For God knew the way
to handle things best.

He brought Ruth to Boaz
        and right from the start,
Boaz knew Ruth
        held a place in his heart.
He gave her protection,
        some grain, and some water
And rejoiced in the way
        she behaved as a daughter.

And before very long,
        Boaz took a stand
And asked sweet Ruth
        for her love and her hand.
Naomi was pleased
        and thanked God for His grace
Each time she beheld
        the joy in Ruth's face.

And even today
        it's good to recall
That family
        is always the best gift of all.
For God gave us families
        to help us be strong
And give us a place
        where we'll always belong.

Read the Book of Ruth in your Bible.

S is for Samson

QqRrSsTtUuVvWwXxYyZzAaBb

When Samson was born
        his mother was told
That Samson would be
        very strong and bold.

An angel told her
        to be aware
That Samson should never
        cut his hair.

For he would be
        a Nazarite
Born to serve the Lord
        and fight.

Samson would be
        a servant, too,
And that's the way
        he lived and grew.

He loved to joke
        and loved to tease,
And he loved God
        and tried to please.

But he went against
        his family's plan
When he chose to marry
        outside his clan.

65

When the marriage ended
    in grief and tears,
Samson was lonesome
    for twenty years.

He met Delilah
    who tried at length
To find the secret
    of his strength.

She would ask
    what made him strong,
And Samson would answer,
    but always wrong.

She'd send for soldiers
    to test his story,
But he was so strong
    and would gain all the glory.

Then, finally, he told her,
    "Just cut off my hair,
And I'll be the same
    as any guy anywhere."

Delilah then made plans
    and cut off his locks,
And that landed Samson
    in Philistine stocks.

Samson was blinded
   and weak as could be,
But God quickly strengthened
   his recovery.

Tied between pillars,
   Philistines everywhere,
Samson found strength
   in more than his hair.

He asked God's forgiveness
   and asked for His might,
To bring God the glory
   and make everything right.

The temple collapsed,
   the arch enemy lost,
And Samson redeemed
   himself at great cost.

So we must remember
   when the Lord plans our way,
Our strength is in Him
   each time we obey.

Read about Samson in Judges 13—16.

T is for Tree

Let's look at the tree
     in the biblical story
And see how it's always
     been part of God's glory.

The first tree we find
     in ancient times stood
In the Garden of Eden
     showing evil and good.

The other tree there
     with the man and his wife,
Was the tree that God planted,
     called the tree of Life.

These trees were the symbols
     of something divine
And all through the Bible,
     trees served as a sign.

There were olive trees,
    with fruit of the vine,
And fig trees to shade you
    at naptime just fine.

There were palm branches, too,
    to be waved with delight,
And sycamore trees
    gave Zacchaeus great height.

Then there's the tree that was cut
    for a manger
Where baby Jesus
    was kept from danger.

And finally, the tree
    on Easter hill
Where Jesus died
    of His own free will.

Yes, the tree is a symbol
    God used to share
His love and truth,
    and constant care.

So if you see a tree
    to climb on or swing,
Lift your voice to God
    and let your heart sing.

*Read about the trees in the Garden of Eden
in Genesis 2.*

U is for Universe

In the beginning,
    in that time long ago,
God made the stars
    and set the moon aglow.

He created the heavens
    and planets and spheres
That we've all gotten used to
    over the years.

This universe
    was God's great delight,
And you can be sure
    He did everything right.

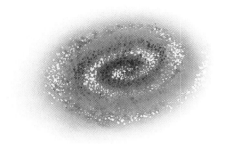

He gave us a place
    full of plants and birds
Where animals gather
    in packs and herds.

He gave us mountains
    to climb and view,
And then He gave us
    some oceans, too.

God was the One
    who knew what we'd need
So He planted the earth
    with every good seed.

He caused things to grow
    in the land and the sea
So that we'd have a place
    to be happy and free.

The universe
    shows God's creative power,
And He made it all
    from the rock to the flower.

So tonight when you look
    at the stars twinkling bright,
Be sure to thank God
    for creating the light.

Read about the universe in Genesis 1 and 2.

V is for Victory

Did you ever find
    yourself in a race
Where you hoped to win
    and be in first place?

Did you ever try
    as hard as you could
To do your best
    and be really good?

Well, if you've tried,
    than you can see
How it feels to score
    a victory.

This very same thought
    is one to apply
When you're thinking of God,
    and here is why.

Every day, when you're
    learning and winning
And trying so hard
    to keep from sinning,

You're trying to please
    your mom and your dad
So that deep in your heart
    you feel really glad.

Well, when you are able
        to do things just right,
Doesn't it always bring joy
        and delight?

So you can imagine
        how God must feel too
When He sees your love
        and the good things you do.

Each time you please God,
        that's surely the key
To living a day
        filled with sweet victory.

Read about victory in 2 Timothy 4:7-8.

W is for Word

Perhaps at home
    or at church, you've heard
That the Bible is known
    as God's holy Word.

When you read the Bible
    or it's read to you,
God gives a great promise
    it's good that you knew.

He says that His Word
    is lasting and true,
And it will dwell always
    inside of you.

He says that it's good
    to do your part,
To carry His Word
    in your very own heart.

So when you read your Bible
    or it's read to you,
Remember God's Word
    will forever be true.

Read Psalm 119:11 for more about God's Word.

X is for Xerxes and his queen, Esther

When Xerxes was king,
    he took a new bride,
And Esther was Queen
    right by his side.

Esther was Hebrew,
    devoted and true,
To God's chosen people
    all her life through.

Because she was favored
    in King Xerxes' eyes,
He listened to Esther
    and considered her wise.

A wicked man
    in Xerxes' own court
Told the King that the Jews
    were a most evil sort.

He wanted to kill Esther's uncle
    as well,
And that's when Queen Esther
    decided to tell.

She asked the King's favor
　　to just hear her out,
And then she revealed
　　all her fear and her doubt.

She spoke of the plot
　　against Mordecai
And defended her people
　　as she uttered her cry.

Xerxes believed her
　　and had Haman destroyed,
Then he honored her uncle
　　and kept him employed.

Esther was brave,
　　a Queen of great beauty,
And she saved her people
　　out of love and duty.

Sometimes it's hard
　　to be brave in all things,
But remember Queen Esther
　　who stood up before kings.

Read the Book of Esther in your Bible.

Y is for You

Though you may not know it,
    God knew from the start,
Each hair on your head,
    each thought in your heart.

He knew you before
    your mom and dad did,
And wanted to make you
    His very own kid.

He gave you your eyes
    to see all that is good,
And He gave you a heart
    to do all that you should.

He gave you your ears
    to hear Him calling,
And gave you strong legs
    to keep you from falling.

He loved you so much
    that He came to earth
To save you from sin
    long before your own birth.

For God is your Father,
      your Friend, and your Guide,
And He wants you always
      to be by His side.

So just take a moment
      to thank Him today
For planning your steps
      and guiding your way.

Read Psalm 139 to find out how much God knows about you.

Z is for Zion

Some cities are special in God's sight
And remind us of His truth and might.
Some are holy, some are rotten,
Some will never be forgotten.

Bethlehem is the little one
Where God chose to have His Son.
Shepherds came and wise men, too,
To see what glory God would do.

Nazareth was Jesus' place
Where He learned and shared God's grace,
Where He taught his friends and neighbors
What God wants from all our labors.

Jerusalem was David's city,
One for whom God wept with pity,
One He wanted to be true
And follow Him each day through.

And some call Zion heaven's place,
The city of God's perfect grace.
Zion is our hope of glory,
The place where we will share God's story.

Wherever you might live right now,
Give thanks and always pray,
That God will bless your home on earth
And help you live His way.

Read Luke 2 to find out about Bethlehem.

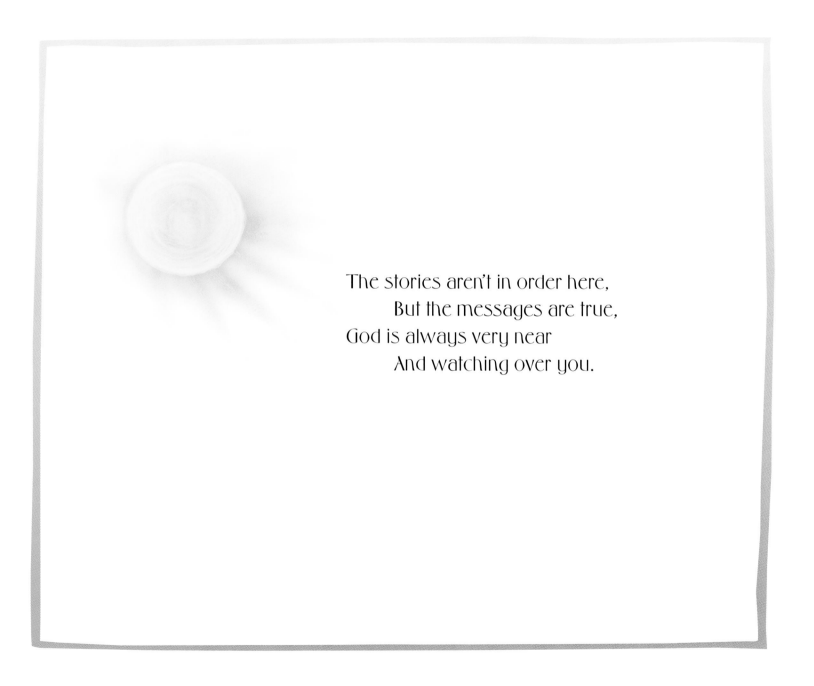

The stories aren't in order here,
　　But the messages are true,
God is always very near
　　And watching over you.

Practice Your Alphabet

A B C D E F

a b c d e f

Practice Your Alphabet

GHIJKLM

ghijklm

N O P Q R S

n o p q r s

Practice Your Alphabet

TUVWXYZ

tuvwxyz

The ABC Bible Storybook

Ages: 4-7

Life Issue: My preschooler needs to learn the alphabet, so by using Bible stories to help teach the letters, I can plant the seeds of faith in my child's heart.

Spiritual Building Block: Faith

Learning Styles

Sight: Watch a video presentation of one of the stories in this book or read the entire story from a different Bible storybook. Talk about the story with your child and ask a few questions based on your child's level of understanding. Zero in on the letter that is associated with this story and review the basic story as you daily review the alphabet.

Sound: Play a simple game. Sing the alphabet song. When you sing the song a second time through, stop at any letter. Ask your child, "What was the story we learned for this letter?" Continue in the same manner until several letters have been covered. On the last time through the song, change the last line to "Jesus always loves me."

Touch: Buy a set of magnetic letters. Place them on your refrigerator and each day have your child choose one letter to be the letter for the day. Read the corresponding story in this book. Then have your child mark the calendar with the letter he or she learned today. As the days pass, go back and review stories and letters that you have already learned.

I have hidden your word in my heart that I might not sin against you.

Psalm 119:11